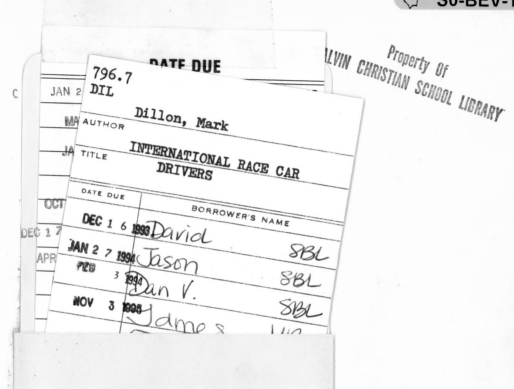

DATE DUE

796.7
DIL

Dillon, Mark
AUTHOR

INTERNATIONAL RACE CAR
TITLE   DRIVERS

DATE DUE	BORROWER'S NAME	
DEC 1 6 1993	David	
JAN 2 7 1994	Jason	8BL
FEB 3 1994	Dan V.	8BL
NOV 3 1998	James	8BL
		Mit

INTERNATIONAL
RACE CAR DRIVERS

The Racing Books

INTERNATIONAL
RACE CAR DRIVERS

MARK DILLON

FRANK HAIGH

Lerner Publications Company ■ Minneapolis, Minnesota

ACKNOWLEDGMENTS: The illustrations are reproduced through the courtesy of: pp. 4, 38, 39, 50 United Press International; pp. 6, 15, Richard George; pp. 7, 26, 27, 33, 35, 36, 41, 42, 45, 46, 47, Phipps Photographic; pp. 8, 12, All American Racers, Incorporated; pp. 10, 21, Sport Photographic; pp. 11, 28, Indianapolis Motor Speedway; pp. 16, 19, General Graphics; p. 17, Fiat, Italy; pp. 22, 24, 29, 30, Pete Biro; p. 25, Vernon Biever; p. 31, The Goodyear Tire and Rubber Company; p. 48, Michael Tee of Motor Sport.

Cover: Phipps Photographic

LIBRARY OF CONGRESS CATALOGING IN PUBLICATION DATA

Dillon, Mark.
International race car drivers.

(The Racing Books)
SUMMARY: Describes the lives and the racing careers of four well-known international race car drivers: Dan Gurney, Mario Andretti, Jackie Stewart, and Emerson Fittipaldi.

1. Automobile racing—Biography—Juvenile literature. [1. Automobile racing—Biography] I. Haigh, Frank, joint author. II. Title.

GV1032.A1D55   796.7'2'0922 [B] [920]   73-22514
ISBN 0-8225-0413-8

Published simultaneously in Canada by J. M. Dent & Sons Ltd., Don Mills, Ontario.

Manufactured in the United States of America.

International Standard Book Number: 0-8225-0413-8
Library of Congress Catalog Card Number: 73-22514

Second Printing 1975

INTRODUCTION

The most celebrated race-car drivers in the world are those who have conquered the fast and treacherous courses of international road racing. Dan Gurney, Mario Andretti, Jackie Stewart, and Emerson Fittipaldi are four such drivers. Most of them are known chiefly for their skills in Formula 1, or Grand Prix, racing. But their experience extends to other classes of automobile racing as well. Mario Andretti, for example, has long been recognized for his winning record in American oval-track racing. During the last few years, however, Andretti has displayed his amazing versatility by competing successfully in international Formula 1 events.

Most Formula 1 racing is conducted on road courses. These road-racing courses, called circuits, have been designed to duplicate the natural driving conditions found on ordinary town and country roads. The circuits are made up of curves and uphill and downhill grades. There may be variations in light and shade along the courses, just as there are on tree-shaded country roads. Sometimes the road surface varies from place to place as well.

An exception to this basic form of Grand Prix racing is known as "round-the-houses" racing. A Formula 1 race of this kind, such as the Grand Prix of Monaco, is actually run through the streets of a town. In this situation, the driver has to contend with additional factors like curbs, telephone poles, buildings, and stray animals. At the same time, he is jockeying for position while traveling at tremendous speeds. Not only is the driver's judgment and driving skill tested, but the car's handling ability and endurance are also put to a severe test.

The cars are Formula 1 cars, which are among the most powerful of auto-racing machines. They are single-seat, open-wheel

The 1967 Grand Prix of Belgium was run on a portion of public road that passed through several villages in a hilly, heavily wooded area.

cars in the entire formula-car division, a division made up of many classes.

In Formula 1, as in other race-car divisions, special recognition is given the driver who has won the greatest number of races during the year. The most coveted award in Formula 1 racing is the World Drivers' Championship. It is the highest honor in what has traditionally been automobile racing's major speed contest. The driver who wins the World Drivers' Championship, therefore, is considered to be the world's foremost race-car driver.

The total number of Grand Prix events conducted each year varies. Of the total number, only a few are *championship* races, the ones that count toward the World Drivers' Championship. Only the first six finishers in each championship race receive

vehicles that have no fenders. There is a strict formula, or set of rules, controlling the cars' weight, design, and engine size. (This formula is subject to change every few years.) Formula 1 racers are the largest and fastest points. Nine points are awarded for a first-place finish, six points for a second-place finish, four points for third place, three points for fourth place, two points for fifth place, and one point for a sixth-place finish. At the end of the season, the driver with the most points is awarded the championship. If there is a tie, the championship is awarded to the driver with the greatest number of total races won. Though nothing more than the title and a trophy are awarded, it is the achievement itself that matters.

Two of the racing heroes in this book, Jackie Stewart and Emerson Fittipaldi, have won the World Drivers' Championship. Though Mario Andretti and Dan Gurney have not received this honor, they have won many Grand Prix events and have also been awarded major titles in other race-car divisions. Regardless of

Emerson Fittipaldi (center) looks forward to his victory toast after winning the 1970 United States Grand Prix. Two years later, he won the World Drivers' Championship.

individual achievement, all four drivers share the belief that Formula 1 racing is the ultimate racing contest. And they have dedicated their lives to winning as many of those contests as possible.

DAN GURNEY

Dan Gurney is one of the few men in auto racing to be successful both at racing cars and at building them. The excellent performance of his cars and his own skilled performance as a driver have been witnessed again and again on the twisting, turning road courses of Europe and America. Dan has always liked road racing better than track racing, but both he and his cars have earned special acclaim at such famous track races as the Indianapolis 500. Though he retired as a race driver in 1970, Dan Gurney has continued to be active in racing as a builder of some of the world's fastest race cars.

Dan Gurney was born in Port Jefferson, New York, in 1931. After he finished high school in New York, Dan moved with his family to southern California. It was there that he became interested in automobile racing. Almost all of the races he went to were track races that featured jalopies, sprint

Dan Gurney

cars, and stock cars. Track racing was very popular during those days of the late 1940s, and races were held several times a week in many locations. Despite track racing's popularity, however, Dan's favorite kind of racing was road racing, which was still quite new in America then. Dan saw auto races of all kinds, but he decided that road racing was what he wanted to do most.

Before starting his racing career, however, Gurney enrolled in college. Four years later, upon finishing college, he went right into the service and was stationed in Korea. When he left the service, 24-year-old Dan Gurney was finally ready to start racing.

With money that he had saved and borrowed, Gurney bought his first sports car, a Triumph TR2. He raced the TR2 in local California races in 1955, and by the end of the year he had moved up to faster cars, such as Porsches and Corvettes. With every race,

Dan's reputation as a fast driver grew. He was soon offered a new Ferrari for driving in the California road races. By 1957, after having won several important races, Dan Gurney was considered to be one of the best sports-car drivers in southern California.

Gurney had accomplished a lot in the two short years he had been racing sports cars. But his greatest ambition was to drive Formula 1 cars, the best among road-racing machines. Dan knew that if his dream was to come true, he would have to go to Europe, where his driving ability could be seen by the big-name factory teams, or car manufacturers. Then, as now, being asked to drive for a factory team was not only a real achievement, but also the road to success for a determined driver. So in 1958, Dan went to Europe, where he drove an independently owned sports car in various competitions. By the middle of 1959, the highly regarded

Ferrari company had become so impressed with Dan's driving ability that they asked him to drive their Formula 1 car.

Driving the Formula 1 Ferrari, Dan Gurney finished second at the 1959 German Grand Prix. But the remainder of the year with Ferrari wasn't very successful for Dan, so he moved to the BRM team—another leading European car manufacturer—and drove their cars in the 1960 Grand Prix competitions. Unfortunately, the BRM team proved to be even less successful than the Ferrari team had been. So for the 1961 season, Dan signed to drive Porsche Formula 1 cars.

The year 1961 was a good one for Dan Gurney, because during that year, he earned enough points in Formula 1 competition to place second overall in the World Drivers' Championship standings. Also in 1961, Dan decided to try English sedan-car racing. At the time, the small and nimble Jaguar sedans were

Dan Gurney (second from left) and his co-driver Stirling Moss are honored in Germany after winning a 1,000-kilometer race in 1960.

the only cars winning the sedan races. But Dan thought that a well-built American sedan could do well against the Jaguars. So he had a large Chevrolet sedan prepared for racing and brought to England. At first, the British just laughed at the American sedan because it was so large. But they stopped laughing when they saw the Chevrolet start to beat their Jaguars.

Back home again in 1962, Gurney raced at Indianapolis for the first time. After seven years of road racing in Europe, the 1962 Indy 500 was to be Dan's first oval-track race. And the car he drove was one of the first rear-engined, European road-racing cars at the Indy Speedway. Dan's car broke down early in the race, however, before he could really demonstrate its worth. In an effort to show Americans the advantages of the European cars, Dan asked English car designer Colin Chapman to bring his rear-engined Lotus car to the 1963 Indy. Although the small European cars were clearly better than the American Indy roadsters, they didn't do well in America at

Gurney drove a rear-engined Lotus car in the 1964 Indianapolis 500. The car started in sixth place but did not finish the race.

first. But by 1965, the rear-engined cars were dominating the speedway at Indianapolis. It was Dan Gurney who was mainly responsible for bringing them to America.

In the meantime, Gurney performed well in other race-car divisions. In 1963, he started the season off by winning the Motor Trend 500, a major stock-car race held at the popular Riverside, California, road course. And by 1964, he had won several Formula 1 and sports-car races in both Europe and America. In 1964, Dan also won the Motor Trend 500 for the second consecutive year.

Dan's greatest dream in racing was to win the World Drivers' Championship in Formula 1. And

Gurney waves to his stock-car fans after winning the Motor Trend 500 in 1966 for the fourth year in a row.

he wanted to win it in a car that he designed and built himself. So in 1964, Dan started work on this project by forming his own manufacturing company—All-American Racers in California and Anglo-American Racers in England. By 1965, Dan was building his first Formula 1 car in his British shop. He named his cars "Eagles" because he was a

very patriotic American. While the Formula 1 cars were being built in England, "Eagle" Indy cars and "Eagle" Formula A cars were being built at the California shop.

In 1967, Gurney won two races in his Formula 1 Eagle. One of the victories was a Grand Prix race in which Dan became the first American driver since 1921 to win a

European road race in an American car. The next year, however, Dan was forced to give up his Formula 1 building project due to financial troubles. He then returned to California to manage his All-American Racers shop. Besides building and racing his own cars, Dan continued to race in other car divisions. In both 1965 and 1966, he had won stock-car racing's Motor Trend 500, making a total of four consecutive wins. Race promoters were soon thinking of renaming the Motor Trend 500 the "Dan Gurney 500"!

In 1967, Dan won several important sports-car races, including the Sebring 12-hour endurance race at Sebring, Florida. Dan's Indy Eagles were expected to perform well that season, but mechanical problems consistently kept them from succeeding. Driving an Eagle in the 1967 Indy 500, Dan led the race for 160 laps. Then, just before the race's end, the car broke down. But despite the failure at Indy, 1967 proved to be a good year for Dan. He won a championship-car race at Riverside, and, co-driving with A.J. Foyt, he won the 24-hour endurance race for sports cars at LeMans, France.

Dan started the 1968 racing season by winning the Motor Trend 500 for an incredible fifth time. Then he concentrated all his efforts on American track racing. He came close to victory at the 1968 Indy 500 when he placed second—his best finish at Indy yet. But more important, one of his Indy Eagles *won* the Indy that year thanks to the driving skill of Bobby Unser. Besides winning at Indy, Dan's Eagles won two other championship-car races in 1968. A year later, Dan barely missed a victory at Indy as Mario Andretti beat him to the checkered flag by mere seconds. But Dan's Eagles did well during the rest of the 1969 season, proving to be a threat in many a race.

By 1970, Dan was anxious to get back to Formula 1 racing. So he went to Europe and drove the McLaren formula cars. He also drove the powerful McLaren sports cars in the 1970 Can-Am Championship—the most spectacular road race in America. Although Dan's Formula 1 racing wasn't very successful that year, he won the first 2 races out of the 10 in the Can-Am series. Meanwhile, Dan's All-American Racers shops were producing some Plymouth Barracudas for the sports-sedan racing in the Trans-Am Championship. And, of course, Dan's shops were still producing the Eagle Indy cars.

At the last race of that 1970 season, a Trans-Am race at Riverside, Dan unexpectedly announced his retirement from race driving. He never achieved his goal of winning the World Drivers' Championship in Formula 1. Nor did he ever win the Indianapolis 500. But in spite of this, Dan Gurney remains one of the all-time greats in auto racing. His performances on the European road courses over the years have been equalled by very few American drivers. His performances on American road courses and oval tracks have earned him the reputation of being among the most versatile American drivers. And his contribution to the world of auto racing through the manufacture of quality racing machines is considerable. Among Gurney's race-winning Eagles, for example, is the car that won the 1975 Indy 500. Gurney builds other kinds of racing cars as well.

Because of his past record as a driver and his continuing involvement as a builder, Dan Gurney has become a living legend in professional auto racing.

Dan Gurney (foreground) in his last race, a 1970 Trans-Am event at the Riverside speedway

MARIO ANDRETTI

Sixteen years after Mario Andretti first raced a car, he won America's most important auto race—the Indianapolis 500. Since then, Andretti has been most widely recognized for his success in Indy-car competition. He has been a big winner in other American race-car divisions as well, racing midget, sprint, stock, and sports cars. Most recently, Mario Andretti has made a name for himself in Formula 1, or Grand Prix, competition. He is indeed a driver who can win any automobile race in any kind of car.

Mario Andretti and his twin brother, Aldo, were born in Montana, Italy, in 1940. Their father was the administrator of a large farm there, which was seized by the Nazis at the outbreak of World War II. During the war, Mario, Aldo, and their sister, Anna Maria, traveled around Italy with their parents as Mr. Andretti looked for other work.

Mario Andretti

He eventually found permanent work in Trieste, Italy, so the family settled there. It was during those years in Trieste that Mario and Aldo watched the road races near their home and dreamed of the day when they could race, too.

In Italy, as in the rest of Europe, all auto racing was called "road racing" because the race courses were modeled after the natural characteristics of public roads. In fact, road races were often held right on public streets that were closed to regular traffic on the day of the race.

During the 1950s, the Italian government started a road-racing program for young boys, called "Formula Junior." Designed to develop champion race drivers for Italy, the program was named for the race cars that were used —small, single-seat formula cars with small Fiat engines. (The cars were miniatures of

An Italian Formula Junior race car

the regular formula cars used in European road racing.) Formula Junior was open to boys 14 years of age and older, but the 13-year-old Andretti brothers were so anxious to join that they lied about their age. On their way home from participating in their first Formula Junior race, Mario and Aldo made up stories to tell their parents. They knew that their parents would not approve of racing, so they kept it a secret.

Both Andretti brothers did well in Formula Junior. But after a few members were injured in crashes, the Italian government had to stop the program. Formula Junior's cancellation was a hard blow for Mario and Aldo, but they decided that it would only be a matter of time before they would be able to race again.

About this time, Mr. Andretti decided to move his family to the United States, where he hoped to find better work and a better life. Although Mario and Aldo were at first disappointed to leave the road racing of Italy, they found a different type of racing to enjoy in America—track racing. The round or oval-shaped dirt tracks of America were quite a change from the paved and winding road courses of Italy. Though it was strange to them, the two boys figured that track racing *was* still racing.

The Andretti brothers' early years in their new home, Nazareth, Pennsylvania, were difficult ones. They had to spend their evenings learning English, as well as keeping up with their regular school studies. But busy or not, they found time to watch American track racing and to figure out how they could become involved in it themselves.

Buying a car, they knew, was the first step. So the brothers worked at a local garage after school to earn extra money. Eventually they saved enough to buy their first race car, a Hudson stock car. Taking turns racing the car in competition, Mario and Aldo kept their activities a secret from their parents, as before. Mario, who stood five feet six and weighed 130 pounds, had a difficult time handling the big car at first. Aldo, who was not much larger, had the same problem. But both brothers managed to overcome the problems created by their small size. In 1959, their first year on the dirt-track circuit, both Mario and Aldo won races in their stock car. The brothers made a good showing until the last race of the season.

During that race, Aldo's car went out of control and crashed into the fence bordering the track. Seriously hurt, he was taken to a hospital to recover. The elder Andrettis were naturally shocked and unhappy when they found out what had happened. But there was nothing they could do to keep their sons from racing.

Mario Andretti is wheeled onto the track for the start of a sprint-car race in 1964.

Mario continued to race cars while Aldo recovered in the hospital. A year later, when Aldo returned to racing, Mario was already a much better driver. Besides racing stock cars, he had started driving midget and sprint cars, too.

By 1964, Mario was driving a sprint car in the United States Auto Club (USAC) racing circuit—the "big league" that could lead a good driver to the Indianapolis 500. Mario's driving was considered to be very wild, but there was no denying that it was very good. Although he didn't win many races during the 1964 season, Mario did receive the notice of many important car owners and sponsors. One important car owner, in particular, had his eye on Mario. He was Al Dean, of Dean Van Lines. Over the years, Dean had sponsored many young drivers who had eventually become Indy champions. Now, in 1964, Dean believed that 24-year-old Mario Andretti also had championship potential, so he offered Mario one of his Indy cars for the 1965 Indy 500. This offer marked the start of Mario's greatest years in racing.

The 1965 racing season was only Mario's second in the big league, but it was the year that the public first glimpsed his great ability as a driver. That year, in his first Indianapolis 500 race, the young rookie finished third behind winner Jim Clark and runner-up Parnelli Jones. He drove many other races that year, but the only race that he actually won was a road race in Indiana. By the end of the season, however, Mario Andretti had placed high enough in the point standings to become the USAC National Champion of 1965. That was quite an achievement for a rookie.

The following year, 1966, Mario again drove for Al Dean. Although he still could not claim a victory in the 500 (he finished

Andretti in his first Indianapolis 500 in 1965. His third-place finish was impressive for a rookie.

to win the Indianapolis 500. But on the 58th lap of the race, his car's right front wheel flew off unexpectedly, forcing him out of the race. He placed 30th overall. Mario then turned his attention to winning his third national title. He drove hard during the remaining months to earn points toward winning the title. By the time of the season's last race, a road race at Riverside, California, Mario was leading in total points. He knew that he could win the title if he placed well in the Riverside race. The race, however, turned out to be a hard-fought battle between Mario and A.J. Foyt—another fierce contender for the title. When Foyt's car broke down during the race, it looked as though Mario would

18th), Mario did well that season. He won his second national championship, this time with eight solid wins behind him.

In 1967, the third year of Al Dean's sponsorship, Mario made another determined effort win. But Foyt came back strong in a borrowed car. Though neither driver won the race, Foyt finished ahead of Mario and thus earned more points. When each driver's total season points were added up, Foyt emerged as the national championship title winner. He had won by only 80 points over Mario, who finished second in the point standings. Mario did have luck in other racing divisions that season, though. He won both the Daytona 500 for stock cars and the Sebring 12-hour endurance race for sports cars.

The 1967 season ended on a sad note. Al Dean, the man who had given Mario his start, died. In order to keep Dean's team of cars active, Mario and his mechanic, the able Clint Brawner, bought and raced them themselves. Mario looked forward to 1968 as a chance to

Andretti (1) leading the pack at Riverside, 1967

better his driving achievements and to forget the bad luck of 1967.

But the 1968 racing season turned out to be a repeat of the previous one. Mario again failed to win at Indianapolis due to car trouble. So he again worked to build up points in an effort to win the title. As in 1967, he had to finish well in the last race of the season in order to win the title. Unfortunately, he only managed to finish third in the race, while Bobby Unser won both the race *and* the national championship.

In 1969, Mario and Clint Brawner sold their team of cars to Andy Granatelli, respected car owner and race sponsor. They had found that the responsibilities of ownership kept them off the tracks too much. After selling the cars, they signed to work for Granatelli's STP organization. Both Andretti and Granatelli were looking for their first win at the Indy 500. So the two men determined to win it together in 1969. During the practice session, however, disaster struck when Mario lost control of the car and slammed it into the wall. Mario was not hurt, but the car was a total loss. The race would have to be run in the spare car, but the spare was found to use more gas than the original car. Knowing that there was a limit on gasoline at Indy, Mario decided he would have to drive slower in order to save the gas he had. Under these circumstances, even a favorable finish looked doubtful. Mario and Andy hoped they would at least *finish* the race.

As the race started, the faster cars pulled ahead into the lead. Mario maintained a con-

Indianapolis, 1969—Mario Andretti's first big win

sistent speed, concentrating on making his gas supply last. Near the end of the 500-mile grind, the faster cars began to drop out with mechanical problems, and Mario soon found himself out in front. When the checkered flag fell, Mario was in first place. It was the hap-piest moment of his life. Andy Granatelli was so excited that he rushed over to Mario in the Winner's Circle and gave him a kiss. Mario went on to finish the best year of his career by winning his third USAC national title.

Mario Andretti during a thoughtful
moment at Indianapolis

Emerson Fittipaldi navigates a road course near Barcelona, Spain.

As racetime nears, Jackie Stewart is strapped into position and his helmet is securely fastened.

In 1967 Dan Gurney and A. J. Foyt were co-drivers of this sports car during the 24-hour race at Le Mans, France.

Since 1969, Mario Andretti has continued to prove his ability by winning not only track races but also road races. In 1970, Andretti won the Sebring 12-hour endurance race for sports cars. And in 1971, he attained his lifetime dream of driving to victory in a Formula 1 car. His first attempt at racing Formula 1 cars had occurred in 1968 when he entered the United States Grand Prix at Watkins Glen, New York, and captured the pole position. Though Mario didn't win the race, he performed remarkably well in his first attempt at Formula 1 racing. Three years later, he drove a Formula 1 car to victory in the South African Grand Prix. In 1971 he also won a California race for Formula 1 cars.

At the end of the 1971 season, Andretti left his partnership with Andy Granatelli. He then teamed with former champions Joe Leonard and Al Unser to drive Indy cars for

Andretti heading for a win in the 1970 Sebring 12-hour endurance race

owner Parnelli Jones in 1972. Besides driving Indy cars, Andretti continued to race sports cars. In 1972 he won the Sebring 12-hour endurance race for the second time in his career. Racing Indy cars again in early 1973, Mario won one part of the Trenton 200 race, while A.J. Foyt won the other part of that two-race series.

Mario Andretti in the lead at a 1974 Ohio road race. He drove a Formula 5000 car.

Mario Andretti has won major races in practically every form of automobile racing— from midget and sprint cars, to stock cars, to Indy cars, to Formula 1 cars. For these achievements, Mario Andretti is recognized as probably *the* world's most versatile race-car driver. It takes skill and absolute devotion to racing to win this honor, and Mario has both of these qualities. Because automobile racing is his life, Mario Andretti will be a major figure in international auto racing for a long time to come.

JACKIE STEWART

When Jackie Stewart won his 26th Grand Prix at Zandvoort, Holland, in 1973, he had won more Grand Prix races than any other race-car driver in history. And when he clinched his third World Drivers' Championship that same year at the Italian Grand Prix, he became an all-time racing great. (Only Juan Manuel Fangio has been Grand Prix World Champion more times.) Jackie Stewart retired in 1973 and ended a career of achievement that few drivers will ever equal.

John Young Stewart was born in the village of Dumbuck, Scotland, on June 11, 1939. Because his father was a Jaguar dealer and an owner of an automobile garage, cars and racing were part of Jackie's life from the start. Jackie's earliest interest in racing, however, was limited to working in his father's garage and watching his older brother, Jimmy, race. From all appearances, it was Jimmy Stewart

Jackie Stewart

who would be the racing champion in the family. Jimmy drove Formula cars for several factory teams and was an excellent driver. But a bad accident at LeMans in the mid-1950s convinced him to quit racing.

While Jimmy Stewart raced, young Jackie developed interests of his own. He especially enjoyed trap shooting. An expert shot and a fierce competitor, Jackie won every trap shooting championship in the British Isles. But when he tried out for the 1960 British Olympic team, the outcome was a crushing disappointment. As Jackie himself put it, "I got thrashed." No one expected it, Jackie least of all. "It was a terrible blow to my ego, but it was the first time I had learned to face disappointment," he recalled later.

Jackie kept up his hobby of trap shooting, but automobile racing began to appeal to him more and more. In 1961, at the age of 22, he started racing in Scottish club races, driving sports cars and sedans. Only two seasons later, Jackie achieved a racing record of 14 wins out of 23 starts. It was obvious that Jackie Stewart was a racing natural.

Among the people who noticed the excellent young driver was Ken Tyrrell, a Scotch lumberman who was also manager of the Cooper Formula 3 team. Tyrrell watched Jackie drive, liked what he saw, and offered him a contract. Jackie accepted. In 1964, Jackie entered 14 Formula 3 races and won 12 of them. This astonishing record earned him three offers to drive for Formula 1 teams in 1965. Jackie chose BRM.

The BRM team had developed an excellent 1.5-liter Formula machine for the 1965 season. In this car, Stewart drove superbly through the tough Formula 1 competition. He scored three second-place finishes, a third, a fifth, a

Stewart driving a Tyrrell Cooper-BMC Formula 3 car in the 1964 Monaco Grand Prix

pionship Formula 1 race and co-drove the Rover-BRM turbine car to tenth place at LeMans. All in all, these were tremendous performances for a rookie driver.

Jackie Stewart started the 1966 season with a BRM car that had been modified from the year before. The new model now had a 2-liter engine. In it, Stewart won the Monaco Grand Prix. Then he tried his hand at American-style racing at Indianapolis. Driving a John Mecom Lola, Stewart led the field of Indy racers for most of the race. Suddenly, with only eight laps to go, the car's oil pressure dropped to zero, forcing Stewart out of the race. At the time of his misfortune, Stewart had nearly an entire lap's distance on the rest of the field—a lead that

sixth—and captured his first Grand Prix victory at Monza, Italy. His total season points earned him *third place* in the World Drivers' Championship standings for 1965. In addition, Jackie took first place in a non-chamis a rarity at Indianapolis. In spite of his loss at Indy, Jackie looked forward to another good season on the Grand Prix circuits.

But back in Europe, during the Belgian Grand Prix, Jackie's career almost came to a tragic end. He was taking a fast curve on the treacherous Spa course in a rain shower when his car spun off the road and crashed into a fencepost. Though Jackie suffered only minor injuries, he spent a terrifying half hour trapped in a cockpit full of engine fuel. Jackie's close brush with death made him a very vocal critic of the unsafe conditions on many Grand Prix courses. Since then, he and other drivers have pushed hard for safety improvements on nearly all the Grand Prix road courses. Through their efforts, the dangerous Spa course has been closed altogether.

Jackie resumed Formula 1 racing in 1966 after recovering from his injuries. But the success he had enjoyed in 1965 was no longer with him. BRM introduced a new engine, called the H-16, and it proved to be unreliable. Consequently, Jackie's race finishes were not good that season.

Stewart's only real success in 1966 and 1967 came from driving Formula 2 cars for his old friend, Ken Tyrrell. The car he drove was one of a whole fleet of Formula 2 cars developed by Tyrrell. They had French Matra chassis and Ford engines. In 1967, Jackie decided to leave BRM to work full-time with Tyrrell in developing a new Formula 1 car for the 1968 season.

The efforts of Stewart and Tyrrell resulted in the Formula 1 Matra, a racing winner. At the Nürburgring, site of the German Grand Prix, Jackie made a stunning performance in

Stewart finishing in first place at the 1968 German Grand Prix

ahead of the second-place car. That season he was a main contender for the World Championship, even though he had missed three earlier races on account of a broken wrist. At the final Grand Prix race of the season, Jackie Stewart and Graham Hill battled it out for the championship. Stewart lost, and Hill became World Champion. But Jackie had shown everyone that he, Tyrrell, and Matra, the French manufacturer, were a winning combination.

In 1969, everything went right for the Matra team. In a rare showing, Jackie won 6 of 11 Grand Prix races to capture his first World Championship. He defeated runner-up Jacky Ickx by a wide margin of points—63-37. The only dis-

the Matra. In Grand Prix competition, races are usually decided by mere seconds. But at the Nürburgring in 1968, Jackie Stewart finished *four minutes*—nearly seven miles—

appointment of the 1969 season was a second-place finish at the Nürburgring, Jackie's favorite course.

By the end of 1969, Tyrrell and Stewart had had two highly successful seasons with the Formula 1 Matra. But no sooner had they started to enjoy their triumphs than the French Matra manufacturer announced an unusual decision. Because they wanted to field an all-French team for 1970, Matra decided to withdraw their cars from the Tyrrell team. Naturally, the decision was a great disappointment for Ken and Jackie. It meant that they would have to work at least one entire season on developing and perfecting a new car. And that's what they did. In the few months between the 1969 and 1970 seasons, Ken and Jackie searched for a new chassis that would provide a solid framework for a competitive new car. They chose the untested March chassis, combined it with the proven Ford engine, and kept their fingers crossed.

The March-Ford was ready for the first race of the 1970 season, the South African Grand Prix. No one on the Tyrrell team really knew what to expect from the car during its first race. But the March-Ford surprised everybody by finishing third. Then, at the Spanish Grand Prix, Stewart drove the car to first place after leading the race from start to finish. The March-Ford's good luck was not to last, however. Except for second-place finishes in Holland and Italy, it did not finish another race. Mechanical problems, poor handling ability, and a host of other defects put the March-Ford out of competition. With only three races left in the season, Ken Tyrrell tried out a new chassis that he had designed himself. The Tyrrell-Ford looked competitive, but it did not finish any of the season's three remaining races.

The 1970 season was a disappointment for Jackie as far as his own races went. But more than that, 1970 was a year of personal tragedy —not only for Jackie, but also for the entire racing world. Jackie's two closest friends, drivers Piers Courage and Jochen Rindt, were killed in racing accidents within three months of each other. The deaths of his friends affected Jackie deeply. When another close friend, driver Jimmy Clark, was killed in 1968, Stewart had said, "This is the part of motor racing I dislike most. We are a closely knit bunch of people and we live very much together. Sometimes I think it is a very futile and meaningless business."

Shaken though he was by these events, Jackie Stewart was not a man to let tragedy or defeat overwhelm him. A true professional, he bounced back, and in 1971 he won his second World Drivers' Championship.

In many ways, Stewart's 1971 season was a replay of 1969. He again won 6 of 11 Grand Prixs, and he again finished well ahead of the second-place finisher in the championship

Jackie confers with his team manager, Ken Tyrrell (right), as driver Peter Revson looks on. (Revson died in a racing accident in 1974.)

standings. It was the Tyrrell-Ford that made it all possible. With the Tyrrell-Ford now perfected, and with its driver in top form, Jackie was the odds-on favorite to repeat as World Champion in 1972.

Stewart greets his fans after winning the 1972 United States Grand Prix at Watkins Glen, New York.

Fittipaldi. Though Stewart did have a good season, the total effects of an ulcer, fierce competition with Fittipaldi, and an unexpectedly troublesome car put the championship just out of reach. Stewart finished the season second to Fittipaldi, 61-45.

The 1973 Grand Prix season looked like another Stewart-Fittipaldi battle right from the start. Jackie and Emerson were running neck and neck right through the middle of the season. But then the breaks began to fall Jackie's way. In Holland, Jackie Stewart won his 26th Grand Prix, breaking the previous record of 25 wins set by the late Jim Clark. Stewart went on to capture the German Grand Prix at the Nürburgring for his 27th

Two factors worked against Jackie in 1972 to postpone his third title. One was a painful bleeding ulcer, which caused him to miss the Belgian Grand Prix. The other factor was the tremendous young Brazilian driver Emerson win, in a race that the press called "an effort-less runaway." High finishes put Stewart firmly in the lead for the championship, and at Monza he finally won it all. He was World Driving Champion for the third time, amassing the greatest point total in history— 69. And there were still two races to go in the season. A fifth-place finish at Mosport, Canada, brought Jackie up to 71 points and set the stage for the final race at Watkins Glen, site of the U.S. Grand Prix.

Rumors were circulating before the race that Stewart was about to retire. Jackie did not deny the rumors. "For family reasons, maybe I should stop racing," he admitted during a television interview. "I'll have to go home (after this season) and think about it. It will be the biggest decision I'll make in my life." Although no one knew it, Jackie Stewart had decided several months earlier that he would retire. And since the U.S. Grand Prix was the last race of the 1973 season, Jackie knew that it would be his last professional race. But he did not take part in it. During a practice session at Watkins Glen, Stewart's skillful and dashing young teammate, Francois Cevert, was killed in a mishap. In the tradition of racing, the Tyrrell team withdrew from the race out of respect for their dead teammate. It was only a few days later that Jackie announced his retirement from racing.

Jackie Stewart retired at the age of 34, the finest Grand Prix driver in the world. Though he is out of Formula-car competition, he will continue his involvement in racing as a TV commentator for racing events and as a development consultant for Ford. From all indications, Jackie Stewart will continue to be a vital personality in auto racing for many years to come.

EMERSON FITTIPALDI

He describes himself as "small, methodical, and precise." People who meet him say he is a shy and modest young man with a winning smile. His hobbies include water skiing, soccer and golf, and driving his sleek, powerful racing car. He is Emerson Fittipaldi, the youngest Grand Prix driver ever to win the World Drivers' Championship.

Emerson Fittipaldi was born into a racing-minded family in São Paulo, Brazil, on December 12, 1946. His father, a racing reporter and popular radio announcer, had raced motorcycles as a young man. Even his mother was a motorsport fan. She had raced cars herself during the early 1950s and had once finished sixth in a 24-hour production-car race. Besides their love for racing, the elder Fittipaldis admired the American philosopher Ralph Waldo Emerson and the American president Woodrow Wilson. In

Emerson Fittipaldi

An early photo of Fittipaldi go-karting

honor of these men, the Fittipaldis named their sons Emerson and Wilson.

The Fittipaldi brothers began racing when they had just barely reached their teens. Emerson started racing small motorcycles, while older brother Wilson raced go-karts. At that time, race cars were scarce in Brazil because of the high import tax on automobiles. So instead of automobile racing, go-karting was the popular racing sport. Before long, Emerson switched to kart racing himself. In 1965, his first year of go-kart competition, he won the São Paulo Kart Championship. It was kart racing, Emerson claims, that taught him car control and gave him a feel for racing.

Emerson's ability on the go-kart track became so well known that it attracted the attention of Brazilian car manufacturers. These companies were constantly looking for excellent drivers to race their cars against those of other factory teams. When the Brazilian Renault factory team saw Emerson's racing skill, they offered him their sponsorship, or financial support, in their 850 Gordini. Emerson gladly accepted the offer. In his first outing in the car, Emerson zipped past the team's Number One driver as if *he* were the pro. Said the driver, Pedro de Lamare: "He went past me like he was in a different kind of car, but I tried to follow. I managed one or two turns, then I left the road and crashed just trying to follow Emerson."

In 1967, the same year he began racing Formula Vees, Emerson Fittipaldi won the Brazilian Formula Vee Championship. Formula Vees were very popular in Brazil, so Emerson and his brother, Wilson, started a small Formula Vee factory of their own. During their first year in business, the brothers sold more than 25 cars to eager Brazilian drivers. Among the cars that Emerson and Wilson designed was an amazing twin-engined Volkswagen with a fiberglass body. Nicknamed the "Fittipaldi 3200," the car looked like a VW bug, sounded like a big Porsche 917, and went faster than the best race-prepared touring cars. Endurance was the car's only problem; transmission troubles kept it from ever finishing a race.

Emerson was not discouraged. He continued building cars and racing them, all the while saving his money to go to Europe and race in the big time there. Finally, in 1969, he left for England. In an attempt to break into European racing circles, Emerson bought a Formula Ford and raced it in competition. Three months later his driving skill gained the attention of Jim Russell, a representative of the famous Lotus factory team. Russell was impressed enough to offer Emerson the driver's seat in a Formula 3 for Team Lotus. Fittipaldi accepted, and thus he began his fast rise to the top of the racing world.

In his first year of Formula 3 racing, Emerson drove his Lotus 59 to the Lombank Formula 3 Championship. This impressive achievement earned Fittipaldi an invitation from Lotus to race its Formula 2 car in 1970. But the de Tomaso Formula 1 factory also had its eye on Fittipaldi. De Tomaso offered Emerson a chance to race in *Formula 1* that season. This action, of course, put pressure on Lotus to make Emerson a better offer— and they did. Midway through the 1970 season, team manager Colin Chapman asked Emerson to be the Number Three driver for the Lotus Formula 1 team. Out of loyalty to Lotus, Emerson said yes. So at the tender age of 23, Emerson Fittipaldi began racing against the greatest drivers in the world. He had become a Grand Prix driver!

Fittipaldi remembers driving his first Formula 1 car: "The Lotus 49 was a very heavy car to drive. At the end of the German Grand Prix in 1970, I couldn't even straighten out my fingers, I had been grabbing the steering wheel so hard!" Heavy car or not, Emerson took fourth place in that race and earned his first three championship points.

And then there was Monza, the fast, bumpy, high-banked course that is the site

Fittipaldi driving his Lotus 59 to victory in the Lombank Formula 3 Championship race, 1969

Emerson Fittipaldi in his first Formula 1 race, the 1970 German Grand Prix. He finished in fourth place.

tremely fast curve called La Parabolica. Miraculously, he escaped injury. The next day, during the race itself, the great Austrian driver Jochen Rindt, a close friend of Fittipaldi, crashed at almost the same spot Emerson had. To the horror of the racing world, Rindt was killed. A stunned Fittipaldi realized that Rindt's fate could easily have been his own, and he almost gave up racing then and there.

Two races later, however, Emerson Fittipaldi won the 1970 American Grand Prix at Watkins Glen, New York. In only his fourth Grand Prix race, Fittipaldi swept to a victory that had the racing world in a stir. The 23-year-old youngster had proven that he could race with the best of them—and *win*. It was his victory at

of the Italian Grand Prix. Emerson's experiences there in 1970 almost changed the course of his young career.

While practicing for the 1970 Italian Grand Prix, Emerson crashed his Lotus at an ex-

Fittipaldi had driven in only three Formula 1 races before he won his first race, the 1970 United States Grand Prix.

and so did the team's new driving sensation, Emerson Fittipaldi. But mechanical failures in the new Lotus kept the team out of the championship contest. Driving the Lotus 72C, Emerson did not finish his first two races. At midseason, when the Lotus 72D was introduced, things improved only slightly; Emerson managed a pair of third-place finishes and one second-place finish, but no wins. Fittipaldi finished the season with only 16 championship points, which placed him a distant sixth in the final 1971 World Drivers' Championship standings.

Watkins Glen that convinced Emerson to continue racing.

At the start of the 1971 season, excitement ran high in the Lotus camp. The new model Lotus, called the 72C, looked very promising,

The problems that Lotus and Emerson Fittipaldi had in 1971 did not happen again during the 1972 racing season. For one thing, Fittipaldi's Lotus performed better. The car was now known as the John Player Special (JPS), named after the British cigarette company that had become Emerson's sponsor. With this car, Emerson had a victorious season. He wasn't able to finish the season's first race, the Argentine Grand Prix. But he placed second in the South African Grand Prix and roared home in first place three weeks later in the Spanish Grand Prix at Jarama. (Big brother Wilson, who was racing Formula 1 for the Brabham team, placed seventh at Jarama.) Next came Monaco and a fourth place finish, plus three more championship points. But at the Belgian Grand Prix, Emerson set the pace. He won the pole position at the time trials and went on to win the race itself. Emerson Fittipaldi had become the man to beat in 1972; he and his John

Fittipaldi in the cockpit of his black-and-gold John Player Special

Player Special were a winning combination.

During his next five races, Emerson captured 36 of 45 possible championship points through victories in Great Britain, Austria, and Italy. It was a win at Monza, Italy, that finally clinched the title for him. At 25, Emerson Fittipaldi was the youngest driver ever to win the World Drivers' Championship. And he won it at Monza, where just one year before, he had almost decided to give up racing.

Emerson's joy at Monza was followed by disappointment over the season's last two races. He finished 11th in the Canadian Grand Prix and did not finish at all at Watkins Glen, New York. To Emerson, these performances seemed to take something away from his championship win.

At the start of the 1973 season, he looked like the same old Emerson, winning back-to-back first-place finishes in Brazil and Argentina. Through the first six races of the season, Emerson was very strong. But midway through the season, Jackie Stewart pulled ahead of Fittipaldi in the championship point standings. Fittipaldi watched his chances dim and then fade altogether as Stewart clinched the 1973 World Drivers' Championship.

What happened to Fittipaldi? Accidents, mechanical problems, and personal injuries all blocked his efforts during the 1973 season. Some sports writers were even willing to blame Fittipaldi's troubles on the Lotus "odd-year jinx." Lotus cars had won World Championships in 1968, 1970, and 1972, but had

Emerson Fittipaldi is in first place as the checkered flag waves him over the finish line at the 1973 Spanish Grand Prix.

lost in the odd-numbered years of 1969, 1971, and 1973—Jackie Stewart's championship years. Whatever the reason for his difficulties, Emerson certainly lacked the one ingredient he claims every successful driver must have: luck.

Then, in 1974—another even-numbered year—everything turned around for Emerson. Driving for Team McLaren, he won Grand Prixs in Belgium and in his native Brazil. He also rose steadily in the point standings for the championship. Following the United States Grand Prix, the last Formula I race of the season, Emerson Fittipaldi emerged as the world driving champion for the second time in his career.

What does Fittipaldi see in his future besides more Grand Prix racing? "I would like to try racing in the Can-Am and at Indianapolis—but only to see what everyone's talking about. . . ." When he is through racing, Emerson says he would like to build a competition car with his brother, Wilson. If he ever gets around to doing that, Emerson Fittipaldi will have come full circle: from garage jockey to World Drivers' Champion and finally back to the garage—where it all began not so many races ago.

BOOKS IN THIS SERIES

DRAG RACING
ICE RACING
MOTORCYCLE RACING
ROAD RACING
SNOWMOBILE RACING
TRACK RACING
AMERICAN RACE CAR DRIVERS
INTERNATIONAL RACE CAR DRIVERS
THE INDIANAPOLIS 500
THE DAYTONA 500
MOTORCYCLES ON THE MOVE

*We specialize in publishing quality books for
young people. For a complete list please write:*

Lerner Publications Company
241 First Avenue North, Minneapolis, Minnesota 55401